C000143059

The right of Judy Rose to be identified as the author of this
work has been asserted in accordance with Section 78
of the Copyright, Designs and Patents Act 1988

The book cover is copyright to Judy Rose

This book is published by
Grosvenor House Publishing Ltd
Link House
140 The Broadway, Tolworth, Surrey, KT6 7HT.
www.grosvenorhousepublishing.co.uk

This book is a work of fiction. Any resemblance to
people or events, past or present, is purely coincidental.

A CIP record for this book
is available from the British Library

ISBN 978-1-83975-778-5

For Paul

with all my love

How life has changed
Since we were young.
So many ways to be.
We've got the choice
If we don't want
To grow old gracefully.

Some think that we are 'over the hill'...
Well, we have news for you!
From where we're standing,
We have got
A really splendid view.

A great philosophy of life,
A truth that's universal:
You have to make each minute count;
Life's not a dress rehearsal.

Never too old to learn new skills,
And such exciting news,
To find we're now quite brilliant at
'The Art of the Afternoon Snooze'.

A little deafness may creep in
Once we are not so youthful.
But then, selective hearing
Can be extremely useful.

Not so young... yet full of fun.
I think we can conclude
That age is not a number;
It's just an attitude.

Senior Moments will occur,
But are we bothered?
Never!
It's just our age,
No need to rage.
We're all in this together.

'Time passes, and now comfort
Will dictate our fashion tastes.
We see the point of nice flat shoes,
And elasticated waists.

Life's voyage of discovery
Is never ever done,
So don't stop being curious
And you'll be forever young.

In later life, we've learned some things
We wish we'd learned before.
Now older, wiser, we don't sweat
The small stuff anymore.

We will be seen.
We will be heard.
We do not do submission.
We've been there, done that,
Seen it all.
So look, respect,
And listen.

They say the mirror never lies,
But we know very well,
That mirrors can be quite two-faced
And exaggerate like hell.

We're versatile, adapt to change,
Embrace new trends;
Too right!
Though sometimes yearn
For coffee shops
Where the choice was
Black or White.

A busy life can often mean
Suppressed creative flair.
So now's the time to show the world
Your genius laid bare.

The mind and body differ so.
It's one of life's great tricks.
Outside: a Senior Citizen.
Inside: still thirty-six.

For some, the key to happiness
Is simply home sweet home.
And time to just luxuriate
Within your comfort zone.

Some days we know
Our 'get up and go'
Will carry us along.
Some days we fear
It's pretty clear
Our 'get up and go'
Has gone.

When looking at our faces,
Please don't misread the signs.
Not crow's feet and not wrinkles,
But life-lived laughter lines.

Why not throw caution to the wind;
Act quirky as can be.
Exploit the 'oldies' loophole'
That's called
Eccentricity.

The fact that we are ageing
Doesn't bother us at all.
It's just the bloody side effects
That drive us up the wall!

Laughter's the best medicine,
As we are often told.
And the day that you stop laughing
Is the day that you grow old.

Retirement:
No alarm clock.
No daily worklife drill.
Your days are finally your own,
Your diary yours to fill.

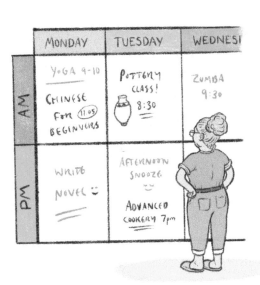

To clarify how things are now,
Compared to way back when...
It's much less
'Rock Around the Clock'
And much more
'Snooze at Ten'.

No point in fighting 'turkey throat';
A battle no-one wins.
So when you get it in the neck,
Just take it on the chins.

By later life, we've learned so much,
Although we must admit...
Remembering exactly what
Is the really tricky bit.

High time to re-invent yourself,
Discover the new you.
And dare to do those crazy things
You've always longed to do.

Of course we drink responsibly,
And this drink leads the way.
Those juniper berries in the Gin
Are one of our five-a-day.

At last, the thing you've longed for;
You've all the time you need,
To get to grip with all those books
You always meant to read.

Now more 'mature', we know our worth;
We're priceless and unique.
With every year our value grows,
Just like a fine antique.

Who knew the inspiration
And joy that it would bring,
The day that you discovered
Your gift for gardening.

Do not treat failing eyesight
As a flaw or imperfection.
It's nature's way of saving you
From the sight of your reflection.

We've made peace with our 'wobbly bits'.
They rarely cause us grief.
If only they would just keep still
Each time we brush our teeth.

Two keep each other's secrets.
It's easier than it seems.
If we cannot remember them,
How can we spill the beans?

Maturing has such bonuses.
A huge one has to be
Not worrying what others think.
It really sets you free.

Never too old for a bucket list
Of things you want to do.
Never too old
To have a dream
And make that dream
Come true.

Remember, with each passing year,
As you turn another page,
The more important it becomes
To never act your age.

Agreed! You're no spring chicken,
But let there be no doubt...
Inside's a party person
Just dying to get out.

We older models know what's what.
We're sassy, savvy, brave.
We've earned the right
To speak our minds
And also misbehave.

You're talking to yourself a lot.
But are you mad?
No way.
And what is more,
You quite agree,
With everything you say.

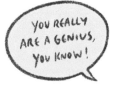

With age, some people modify
The way they live and act.
But embarrassing your children...
You're never too old for that.

We must, of course,
Stay fit, and keep
Decrepitude at bay,
By making sure
We factor in
Some exercise each day.

The Internet.

Oh, what a boon.

Beyond our wildest dreams.

Except when

'Password Incorrect'

Appears upon our screens.

Some goals need modifying
And tweaking, just a touch.
To rise AND shine, some mornings,
Is asking way too much.

A precious gift of later life,
To make your world complete,
Is to hear, the second time around,
The patter of tiny feet.

At any age and stage of life,
The best advice to give,
Is 'seize the day'
And grasp each chance
To love, to laugh,
To live.

With age comes newfound confidence;
We like to stand our ground.
We're tired of rules,
Won't suffer fools,
AND WON'T BE BOSSED AROUND.

When we were younger,
'Happy Hour'
Of course meant half-price booze.
But now it's tea and biscuits
When we've woken from our snooze.

We've loads of clothes from way back when
That fit, and we still wear.
The fact they're mainly
Hats, gloves, scarves
Is neither here nor there.

Our days start in soft focus;
A dream-like mist,
And next...
We squint and grope around a bit
Until we find our specs.

Okay, we may be adults,
But we should never hide
The part of us
That's young at heart
And the child that's still inside.

We thank our lucky stars for friends
Whose interest never wanes,
While we report, describe, bemoan
Our ailments, aches and pains.

The joy of retail therapy
Then lunch,
But best by far,
Is all the fun had afterwards
When playing
'Hunt the Car'.

The real point of a birthday
Is clear,
Make no mistake.
It's Mother Nature telling you
You need to eat
More Cake.

So much to love in later life,
And so say all of us.
We will not be defined by age
And we're still
FABULOUS.

Acknowledgments

I am lucky enough to have two wonderful sons, Oliver and Alexander, who have always been there to encourage, praise and offer advice.

I am especially indebted to Oli, who is also my brilliant Social Media Mentor. It is he who encouraged me to put my poetry on FaceBook, set it all up for me, and has been holding my hand every step of the way.

Daniel Weisz, my gifted young illustrator, has enhanced my words in a way I could never have imagined. With his incredible talent, brilliant sense of humour and endless patience, he has brought a wonderful new dimension to each and every one of my verses.

And last but by no means least... all my love and thanks to my wonderful husband Paul, who has been my editorial consultant and proofreader for many years and has encouraged and supported me in every way possible.

Judy Rose started writing poetry many moons ago when she realised she needed an outlet to express her experiences of the ups and downs of motherhood, unsuccessful attempts at being a Domestic Goddess and the fruitless pursuit of acquiring the body of Elle MacPherson.

With the passing of time, she turned her attention to writing about Mid-life Moments, and before she knew it, she was reflecting on the many cheerful aspects of being a Vintage Model as opposed to a Supermodel!

Follow Judy on:- https://www.facebook.com/womans.world.observed.

Daniel Weisz studied Illustration at the University of Westminster. He now lives in Seaford in the Southeast of England with his lovely wife Cara and their two little boys, Lenny and Ned, not forgetting their small furry child Peggy-Sue (the Cavapoo). Daniel produces artwork for a wide variety of clients as well as his own range of cards, prints and gifts.

CPSIA information can be obtained
at www.ICGtesting.com
Printed in the USA
LVHW071621081021
699946LV00018B/479